CHICAGO

A Picture Book to Remember Her by

CRESCENT BOOKS
NEW YORK

Until the 1830s Chicago was still a minor trading post situated at the swampy river mouth near the southwestern tip of Lake Michigan. By using its location, as a water gateway from Lake Michigan, Chicago developed to its present position as the second most important and populous city in the United States, and one of the richest industrial and commercial complexes in the world.

In 1803 Fort Dearborn was built to protect merchant interests, but it was destroyed by the Indians in 1812, and all but one of its military and civilian population were killed. The Fort was rebuilt in 1816, and outside the walls a cluster of log cabins and shacks grew up, but this time the settlement attracted little attention from the Indians.

Illinois, with most of its population in the central and southern regions, became a state in 1818. In 1837, with a population of 4,200, Chicago became a city. In 1848 the completion of the Illinois and Michigan Canal, linking the Great Lakes and Mississippi systems, fulfilled Chicago's potential as a major port.

Together with water-borne traffic, the railroad became one of the major freight carriers when two westbound lines were connected, in 1852. By 1856 it had become the nation's chief rail center. Chicago had emerged as the Mid West's major city by 1880, with a population of 500,000. Native U.S. and northern European immigrants poured in attracted by the promise of work in the factories.

Catastrophe struck in 1871 after a long, hot summer and autumn when, according to legend, Mrs. O'Leary's cow kicked over a lantern in her barn. The resulting fire spread rapidly and raged for two days; nearly 300 people died, 90,000 people were made homeless and a third of the city's 15,000 buildings were destroyed. The damage was estimated at 200 million dollars, and aid poured into Chicago from all over the world. The Great Fire was not the only disaster; in 1903 another fire in the Iroquois Theatre killed over six hundred adults and children.

After the Great Fire, rebuilding began in earnest and a new, talented breed of architect came to prominence. One of these was William LeBaron Jenney, who is considered to be the father of the modern skyscraper. Today, Chicago houses some of the world's tallest skyscrapers, and Sears Tower is the world's tallest building, standing 1,468 feet high. Not so tall, but still impressive, are the Standard Oil Building and the John Hancock Center, locally known as Big Stan and Big John. These three buildings dominate the skyline that overlooks Lake Michigan, where yacht marinas, imaginative parks and sandy beaches line the shore.

Chicago's "Magnificent Mile", a stretch of Michigan Avenue north of the Chicago River, can, indeed, only be described as magnificent, with its excellent examples of both old and modern architecture. It begins with the Wrigley Building on one side and Tribune Tower, laced with stone from famous structures all over the world, on the other. Trees and wide strips of grass separate the art galleries and stores that line North Michigan Avenue. Further up the road is the Water Tower which, along with the pumping station across the road, was the only buildings left standing after the Great Fire. In total contrast to Water Tower is Big John, the 100-story John Hancock Center, housing both offices and apartments. The Lindbergh Light, the searchlight on top of the Playboy Building behind the John Hancock Center, was once a beacon for airplanes and ships on the Lake. Where the Magnificent Mile ends the Gold Coast, one of the most perfect residential areas, with splendid views of beaches and lakes, begins.

Chicago, however, has also had its dark side. It was the home of some of the world's most infamous gangsters, including, among others, Al Capone, Johnny Torrio and Dion O'Banion; their story one of death and corruption. During Prohibition, Torrio, Capone and O'Banion gained a monopoly of the illegal alcohol business, and this proved extremely profitable. They became too big for anybody to touch on either side of the law. But due to gangster rivalry both Torrio and O'Banion were murdered, and Al Capone died in prison after being sentenced to 11 years for income tax evasion.

Chicago is now one of America's safest cities, and possibly more exciting than any other. Chicagoans are proud of their city; they have the world's tallest building, the biggest airport and the best hotels. The city has a financial center that almost rivals New York, as well as the stockyards, and the Merchandise Mart. It is the biggest railroad center in the world, it produces almost as much steel as Pittsburgh and it is the largest port on the Great Lakes. Chicago was meant to impress, and it certainly succeeds.

Facing page: the Marc Chagall mosaic in First National Bank Plaza, Chicago.

Aerial views of Chicago showing North Lake Shore Drive (right), Sears Tower (below), Northwestern University (bottom right), and (remaining pictures) the downtown area and the rail network beside Grant Park.

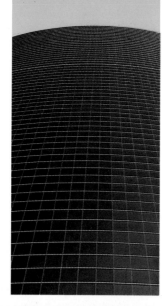

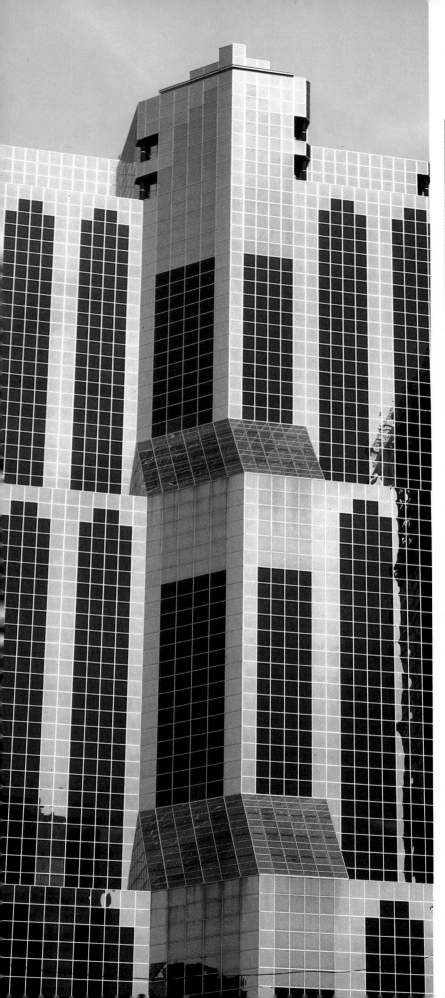

After a third of Chicago was destroyed by fire in 1871, parts of the city were rebuilt with sky-reaching towers that have made it one of the most influential centers of modern architecture in the world.

As America's second largest city, Chicago is surprisingly free of traffic congestion. This is due to a fine highway network (these pages), which is well-served by taxis, and a sophisticated system of public transport, including the elevated "Loop" railroad (below left).

A fairground overlooked by the fabulous Lake Point Tower (top) brings an explosion of speed and color to the downtown area.

As well as fine buildings, such as 333 Wacker Drive (above), Chicago boasts some superb public sculptures, including (left) Calder's *Flamingo*, (facing page right) Claes Oldenburg's *Batcolumn*, (top left) the sculpture outside Adler Planetarium and (bottom left) the famous work created by Pablo Picasso.

Overlooked by the graceful lines of soaring towers, Chicago's city streets (these pages) buzz with a colorful chaos of busy eating houses and garish hoardings.

Twin towers of the most unusual design comprise the Marina City complex of shops and apartments (bottom, far left and below), which overlooks the remarkable "jackknife bridges" (left and far left).

When the city's lights come on (these pages) there appears a magical world of shimmering towers, illuminated fountains and rainbow-colored water.

Numerous yachts and small pleasure craft are sheltered by Chicago's fine harbors (these pages), from which there are superb views of the city's skyline. Burnham Park Harbor (far left) is itself an interesting sight, being bordered on one side by the Meigs Field Airport.

Although Chicago's crime scene has quietened down since the flamboyant gangster days of the 1920s, the police force (these pages) remains well-armed and vigilant at all times.

A number of magnificent fountains adorn many of the public parks and plazas of Chicago. The most notable is Buckingham Memorial Fountain (facing page), which was funded by Kate Buckingham in 1926 and set in Grant Park. Allegedly the largest in the world, it has one jet that reaches a height of 90 feet.

The Chicagoan character is best observed while visiting the city's convivial bars (bottom center) craft shops (below), and colorful markets (remaining pictures), for it is in such public places that the relaxed, creative and essentially sociable nature comes to the fore.

Lake Michigan (these pages) is not only Chicago's loveliest natural asset, it is also the city dwellers' main playground. As well as sailing and fishing, the lake offers miles of beautiful, sandy beaches ideal for swimmers and sun-worshippers.

Among Chicago's many attractions its zoos are popular with visitors of all ages. Shown (left) are the polar bears of Lincoln Park Zoo, while the fine animals (facing page top right, center right and top center left) can all be seen at Brookfield Zoo.

The Wrigley Building (bottom), on the Chicago River's north bank, is one of the fine architectural works visible from the city's most interesting street, Michigan Avenue (remaining pictures).

These pages: views of Chicago, displaying its great variety of architecture. Above: the Art Institute of 1892 and the futuristic Standard Oil Building, (below) Sears Tower and (facing page top left) the 19th-century Water Tower.

It is in "the Loop" (these pages) that the pulse of the city is really felt. This bustling downtown business and shopping district covers less than a square mile and is bounded by an efficient elevated railroad system.

Far right: an aerial view of Michigan Avenue, with the onion dome of the Sheraton Hotel and the splendid, Gothic-style Chicago Tribune Tower in the foreground. Remaining pictures: "the Loop", showing the elevated rail network (bottom center) that has been running since the 1890s.

Chicago is fast becoming known as "Festival City", with various parades and festivals now being staged throughout the year. These imaginative events, such as the Mexican Parade (these pages), allow people of all ages to express creative flair, and fill the heart of the city with music and color.

Some of Chicago's most interesting views can be seen from the water, and there are many boat trips (these pages) offering a convenient and exhilarating way of touring the city.

A part of Chicago's history that will never be forgotten is the gangster era of the 1920s. The most famous name associated with this period is that of Al Capone. These pages: the former hotel where this notorious man had his headquarters while at the peak of his power.

Top left: Southern University.
Bottom left: Soldier Field,
home base of the Chicago Bears
football team. Below, left,
top and top center: the
University of Chicago.
Remaining pictures: Widebold
Hall University Complex.

Right: the Field Museum of Natural History. Below: the Shedd Aquarium. Below right: the Museum of Science and Industry. Remaining pictures: the beautiful Baha'i Temple.

Awesome Sears Tower (right and
far left) is the world's tallest
building and reaches into the sky
for a staggering 1,454 feet.
Below: the John Hancock Tower
dominates the city's glamorous
skyline (remaining pictures).

Lake Michigan (these pages), the largest lake completely within the U.S.A, is often subject to the sudden squalls and large waves associated with inland seas. Chicago's coastal waters, however, are rarely unsafe for sailing and are rich in fish, particularly coho salmon, for which the North Shore is famous.

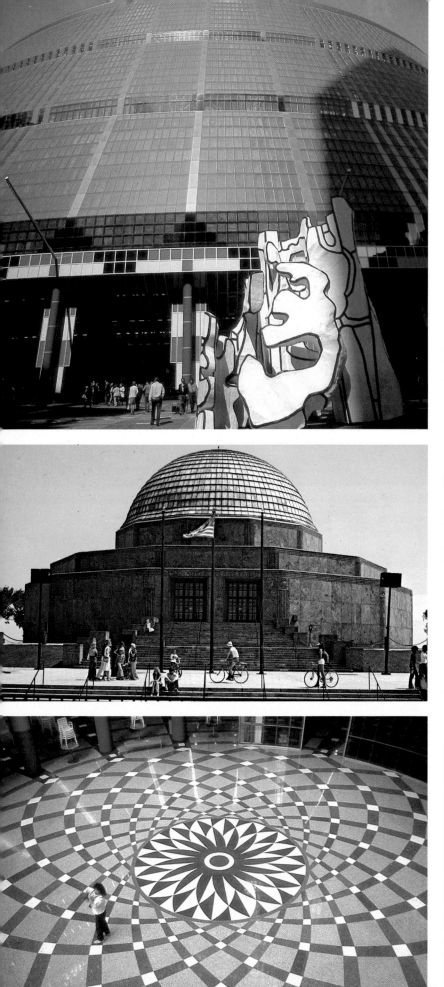

The proud lion (below) and the statue of George Washington (bottom) both stand at the entrance to the superb Art Institute. Below left: Adler Planetarium. Chicago boasts over 30 art galleries, 20 major museums and several cultural centers, one of the most recent being the dynamic Illinois Center (remaining pictures).

55

1992
Chicago World's Fair
Age of Discovery

1992

MARITIM
PEOPLES
*Of the Arctic &
Northwest Coo*

Hall 10

56

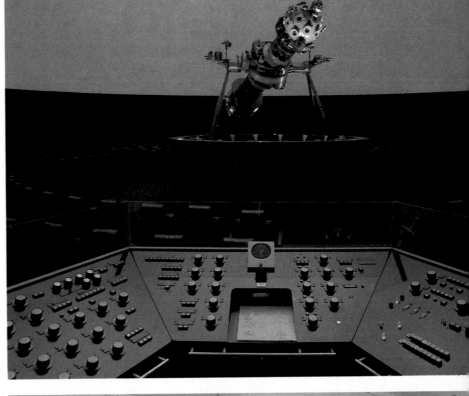

Above: the Polish Museum of America. Top: the Zeiss cosmic projector in Adler Planetarium. Left: a starfighter in the Museum of Science and Industry. Center right: "Nuclear Energy" a bronze sculpture by Henry Moore. Remaining pictures: the Field Museum of Natural History.

The fine statues of Robert Morris, George Washington and Haym Salomon (far left) stand in front of Marina City's twin towers (left and below). Bottom: the Hall of Fame, part of Chicago's massive Merchandise Mart.

These pages: business as usual on the trading floor of the Mercantile Exchange, where millions of dollars can change hands in a matter of minutes. Despite the apparent pandemonium, however, new computer systems (facing page) have greatly eased the flow of such huge transactions.

Unlike many port cities, where the waterfront becomes an untidy jumble of docks and warehouses, Chicago has made an attractive feature of its lakeside and riverside areas (these pages). To turn back and look at the city from a boat in the harbor (left) is to see a great, modern skyline at its best. Overleaf: Michigan Avenue.